A SURVIVOR'S GUIDE TO

BookLife
RAPID
Readers

KU-072-399

THE NIGHT OF THE

ZOMBIES

BY
HERMIONE
REDSHAW

BookLife
PUBLISHING

©2023
BookLife Publishing Ltd.
King's Lynn, Norfolk
PE30 4LS, UK

All rights reserved.
Printed in Poland.

A catalogue record for this book is available from the British Library.

ISBN: 978-1-80155-839-6

Written by:
Hermione Redshaw

Edited by:
William Anthony

Designed by:
Drue Rintoul

AN INTRODUCTION TO BOOKLIFE RAPID READERS...

Packed full of gripping topics and twisted tales, BookLife Rapid Readers are perfect for older children looking to propel their reading up to top speed. With three levels based on our planet's fastest animals, children will be able to find the perfect point from which to accelerate their reading journey. From the spooky to the silly, these roaring reads will turn every child at every reading level into a prolific page-turner!

CHEETAH

The fastest animals on land, cheetahs will be taking their first strides as they race to top speed.

MARLIN

The fastest animals under water, marlins will be blasting through their journey.

FALCON

The fastest animals in the air, falcons will be flying at top speed as they tear through the skies.

Photo Credits – Images are courtesy of Shutterstock.com. With thanks to Getty Images, Thinkstock Photo and iStockphoto. 4–5 – leolintang, LaineN. 6–7 – Gorodenkoff, Paket, freeject.net, Nolte Lourens. 8–9 – Erin Cadigan. 10–11 – Tunatura, Sterling Images. 12–13 – Borkin Vadim, Benevolente82. 14–15 – Lukiyanova Natalia frenta, WAYHOME studio, Mega Pixel. 16–17 – Einar Muoni, Yellow Cat, Smit, Chatham172. 18–19 – Leszek Czerwonka, sirtravelalot. 20–21 – Pressmaster, Fab_1. 22–23 – Tomas Urbelionis, magicoven, donatas1205, photastic. 24–25 – Jeff Wilson, leolintang, FOTOKITA. 26–27 – DarkBird, Pressmaster. 28–29 – Krakenimages.com, HTWE. 30 – leolintang.

CONTENTS

WORDS THAT LOOK LIKE <u>THIS</u> ARE
EXPLAINED IN THE GLOSSARY ON PAGE 31

T BEGINS...

There is no good way to find out the zombie apocalypse has begun.

This will be the first time that you ever see a zombie. Up until now, you probably never imagined they could be real.

Surviving a zombie apocalypse isn't easy. Keeping your cool is the key to staying alive.

You might meet a <u>horde</u> of zombies at any moment. When you do, you're going to need to forget your fear.

If you're lucky, you'll hear about the zombie outbreak before they reach you.

ZOMBIES!

NEWS

You're most likely to find out about the apocalypse on the news. However, a news warning about the zombie apocalypse comes with its own risks.

It's likely that everyone around you will go into <u>survival mode</u>. People in this state can be dangerous. Make sure to stay out of their way.

Instead, find your loved ones. The zombie apocalypse might not be completely horrific with family and friends around you!

SPOTTING A ZOMBIE

You will only have a split second when the panic starts. You will have to work out if someone is a human or a zombie very quickly.

Knowing how to spot a zombie could mean the difference between life and death!

Zombies don't care about getting injured. Most zombies will be bruised or bleeding.

EYES

Zombies have pale, <u>bloodshot</u> eyes.

VOICE

If someone can say more than just, "BRAINS," they aren't a zombie... yet!

WALK

Zombies walk very slowly. They often drag one leg behind the other.

HIDEOUT HUNTING

You don't stand a chance of surviving without a decent hideout.

Avoid hiding out in a small place with only one exit. You don't want to be stuck in a basement with no way out when the horde finds you.

You could find a hideout that is as strong as a castle. However, if it's in the wrong place, you'll end up dead.

The perfect spot is somewhere near to food and clean water. A farm with its own well would work.

You will need to make sure any new base is clear of the undead.

If there are too many zombies inside, do not risk it. Keep looking until you find somewhere el...

NOT HERE!

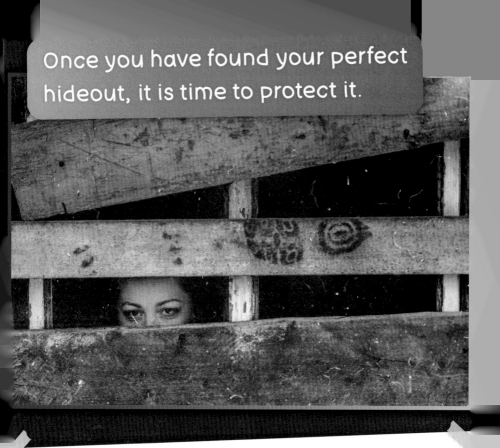

Once you have found your perfect hideout, it is time to protect it.

1. Put up fences and barbed—wire around your base.

2. Board up every window and doorway.

3. Leave a few exits open in case you need to escape.

4. Have people on <u>lookout</u> at all times.

KNOW THE AREA

It is important to know what's around you.

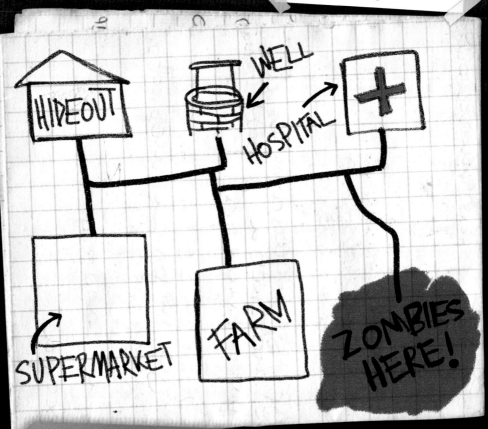

HIDEOUT

WELL

HOSPITAL

SUPERMARKET

FARM

ZOMBIES HERE!

When you feel confident enough, head outside with a pen and paper. Map out how you will get to places for food, weapons and other supplies.

Knowing where to get food, water, weapon and medicine could save your life.

Do not try to take all the nearby food and medicine back to your hideout. If you do, your hideout might become a <u>target</u> for other survivors.

SUPPLIES

You are going to spend lots of time getting supplies. You will always need to be on the lookout for things that can help you.

Fresh food will not last long during a zombie apocalypse.

Turn to tinned food after all the fresh food is gone. Tinned food can stay fresh for a number of years.

Save seeds from fruit and vegetables. Then, you can grow your own!

MEDICINE

Medical supplies are very important, but most people don't know how to use them properly.

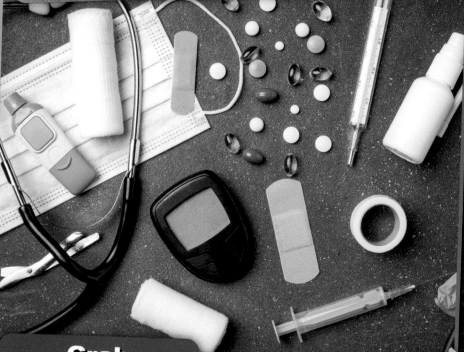

Grab bandages, anti-bacterial wipes and anything else you think you might need.

Try to find a doctor to join your group. Otherwise, stick to what you know.

KEEPING IN CONTACT

No one will deliver the post with zombies everywhere. There will also be no power for phones or computers.

Whistles or walkie-talkies can help you to contact your group if you are far away.

WEAPONS AND TOOLS

Food and supplies are very important. However, you will need to fight off the zombies to get to them.

The best weapons are easy to use and can clear any number of zombies out of your path.

Don't expect a machine gun to appear in the street. Search for tools you can easily find. Such weapons include:

GARDENING TOOLS
SHOVELS
RAKES

KITCHEN SUPPLIES
PANS
ROLLING PINS

SPORTS EQUIPMENT
CRICKET BATS
GOLF CLUBS
HOCKEY STICKS

BE RESOURCEFUL

You can't be too picky when faced with an oncoming horde of zombies. Grab the nearest thing that works.

Stray bits of wood and large stones can make decent weapons. They might just save your life.

Don't forget regular tools...

A hammer and lots of nails can protect your base.

A crowbar will get you into shops with stuck doors.

A torch or candle will help you see at night.

Be careful not to alert zombies with too much light!

DEFENDING YOURSELF

So, the time has come to fight your first zombie. If you're lucky, you will have had time to prepare.

If you've been less lucky, you might only just be realising the apocalypse has begun as you come face to face with a zombie.

AVOID THE MOUTH

One rule is more important the all the res
when fighting a zombie. Avoid the mouth

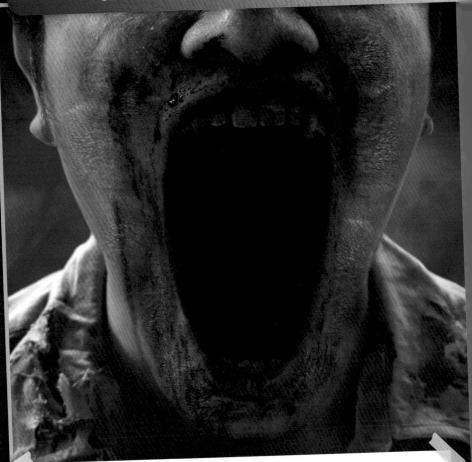

If you're bitten by a zombie, it doesn't
matter if you win or not. You're going
to turn into a zombie. Game over.

ZOMBIES CANNOT SWIM

Zombies can barely walk, let alone swim. Trick your zombie into some deep water, such as a swimming pool, river or pond.

The zombie should be stuck splashing about in the water for a long time.

When you cannot defeat a zombie by being smart, you will have to attack it.

AIM HERE!

A zombie's brain is the only thing that keeps it walking around. You must aim for a zombie's head to stop it once and for a

LIVING IN THE
ZOMBIE APOCALYPSE

Life in the zombie apocalypse can be quiet and lonely. Hiding from zombies can get very boring, even in a group.

To avoid this fate, make sure you have a hobby.

Do anything that takes your mind off the apocalypse. Write stories, practice sports or play games.

Make sure your hobby is not too loud, though. You don't want nearby zombies to hear you!

SURVIVING THE ZOMBIE APOCALYPSE

Life in the zombie apocalypse might not be too bad if you follow this guide. Should any zombies come calling, you will know just how to fight them off.

GLOSSARY

anti-bacterial able to kill germs

horde a large number of zombies that move in a group

lookout when someone is keeping watch for zombies and danger

survival mode when a person automatically starts doing whatever necessary to survive

target an object of attention or attack

undead someone who is dead, but is still moving around like they are alive – in other words, a zombie